Contents

What Is It?

HOUGHTON MIFFLIN   BOSTON

Printed in China

ISBN-13: 978-0-618-93225-2
ISBN-10: 0-618-93225-9

1 2 3 4 5 6 7 8 9 SDP 15 14 13 12 11 10 09 08

2

Look at the Tracks

by Becky Manfredini

Look at the tracks.
What can it be?
Did a great big dog
run here by me?

Look at the tracks.
What can it be?
Did a big fat pig
walk here by me?

Look at the tracks.
What can it be?
Did a young red frog
hop up to me?

Look at the tracks.
What can it be?
A cute gray cat
came up to me!

Words to Know

glad   fast

flops   swims

slips   rest

later   great

stands

Story Word

tracks

Animal Tracks

by David Neufeld

illustrated by Janet Montecalvo

mouse

Look who is here. It runs
fast. It makes little tracks.
It is glad to get a bug.

alligator

Look who is here. It slips up from the water. It flops on sand to rest. It makes great big tracks. What swims past?

10

heron

Look who is here. It stands
on tall legs. It makes tracks in
the soft sand. What can it see?

11

raccoon

Look who is here later. Look at its tracks. How many tracks did it make?